MAKE IT HAPPEN

A WOMAN'S GUIDE TO TAKING CHARGE IN BUSINESS

By Shraddha Agarwal

Qurate
quratebooks.com
Because everyone has a story to tell

Book Creation Services

by

BookMyStory

It's time to tell your story

www.bookmystorypublishing.com

A venture of

R&S Enterprises

MAKE IT HAPPEN
A Woman's Guide to Taking Charge in Business
Shraddha Agarwal

Published in 2024

© Published by

Qurate
qouratebooks.com

Qurate Books Pvt. Ltd.
Goa 403523, India
www.quratebooks.com
Tel: 1800-210-6527, Email: info@quratebooks.com

ISBN: 97-893-58986-54-9

DEDICATION

To the courageous, compassionate and powerful women who chase their dreams and turn them into reality.

PREFACE

In 1999, amidst the lively streets of Mumbai, with an architecture degree in hand and a heart full of dreams, I embarked on a new chapter of my life. Marrying and moving to this vibrant city, I embraced both the roles of a wife and a dreamer, eager to see where this new journey would lead. As years rolled by, engrossed in family life, I couldn't pursue my qualification and decided to shift gears. My heart swayed to varied melodies - from the grace of art to the allure of fashion, from the lens of photography to the limitless horizons of travel. But with every endeavor, I found myself at a perplexing junction. My passions were many yet turning them into a sustainable business seemed like an insurmountable challenge.

Over 18 long years, it dawned upon me: while I was an expert in my chosen fields, the entrepreneurial mindset was the jigsaw piece I was missing. This realization became my turning point. Determined that no other woman should tread this meandering path, I channeled my experiences and emerged as a business coach, uniquely tailored for women entrepreneurs.

INTRODUCTION

This isn't merely my tale, but a sentiment echoing amongst countless gifted women. We wear many hats, transitioning seamlessly from homemakers to dream chasers. Yet, the bridge from passion to a successful enterprise seems elusive.

With every story of triumph and each lesson learned, I've woven them into this book: a guide, a mentor, and a beacon for every woman entrepreneur out there. If you've ever felt tethered by your fears, limited by societal expectations, or overwhelmed by the unknown, this book speaks to you. 'Make It Happen' is more than just a title; it's a clarion call to break free from self-imposed shackles.

Rather than offering cookie-cutter solutions, this book provides potent strategies, drawing from global expertise and my personal odyssey. It doesn't peddle magical cures but shares the hard-earned wisdom that propelled me to confront adversities head-on, crafting the success I cherish today. Dive deep into these strategies, embrace their core, and actualize them. For, this book unveils its treasures to those fueled by genuine passion and an unwavering commitment to evolution.

Let this be your guiding light, your manual, your mentor, and your most trusted ally on this exciting journey of entrepreneurship. Embrace the lessons, celebrate each milestone, and remember, every challenge is but a stepping stone to success.

So, dear reader, as you embark on this transformative journey with 'Make It Happen', know that a new chapter awaits you. Let's craft this story of empowerment, fulfillment, and unparalleled success, hand in hand. Make your dreams happen, for they've waited long enough.

Table of contents

Part 1

JOURNEY

CHAPTER 1

OBSTACLES OF WOMEN ENTREPRENEURSHIP

As an international business coach, I encounter women entrepreneurs expressing the following challenges frequently:

Challenge 1: Struggle for time

We all know how tricky it is to manage time as a woman entrepreneur. I mean, we're expected to be superheroes, juggling business tasks, family obligations, and personal needs. It's like trying to squeeze 30 hours into a 24-hour day. Every minute counts and finding that balance feels like a constant battle. Isn't it overwhelming and frustrating? And sometimes makes me wonder if I'll ever catch a breath!

Challenge 2: Balancing responsibilities

We have a never-ending to-do list, and everything feels equally urgent and important. We want to be there for our loved ones, grow our businesses, and take care of ourselves, but how do we decide what gets our attention first? It's like being torn in a million different directions, constantly questioning if we're making the right choices. We are always finding that perfect balance between work and life. We often find ourselves blending the two, trying to find harmony and synergy. But let's face it, it's not always.

Challenge 3: Guilt and Self-Care

Ah, guilt, my old friend. It seems to follow us everywhere. We feel guilty when we're working and not spending time with our families, and guilty when we take time off and think about the business. It's a never-ending cycle of self-doubt and feeling like we're letting someone down. And during it all, we often forget to take care of ourselves. We put everyone else's needs before our own, neglecting our well-being and burning out in the process.

Challenge 4: Setting boundaries

Setting boundaries can be tough, especially when we're passionate about our businesses. We want to go above and beyond for our clients, team members, and customers. But that sometimes means sacrificing our personal lives and blurring the lines between work and home. It's hard to say no or establish clear boundaries when we fear missing out on opportunities or letting people down. It takes courage and conviction to stand up for us and create a healthy work-life balance.

Challenge 5: Showcasing skills

Society still has certain expectations of how women should behave, and it can be challenging to break free from those norms. Building brand awareness, establishing credibility, and differentiating ourselves in a crowded market can be a significant challenge. But remember, building a brand is about owning your uniqueness and letting your voice be heard. It's about creating an authentic and consistent brand experience that reflects our values and connects with our customers on a deeper level. Being assertive and confident doesn't make you less of a woman, it makes you a powerful entrepreneur.

Challenge 6: Client acquisition

You know that feeling when you pour your heart and soul into your business, but struggle to reach and connect with your ideal clients? It's frustrating, isn't it? We want to share our products or services with the world, make a difference, and create a loyal customer base. But sometimes, it feels like we're shouting into the void, wondering if anyone is listening. The challenge lies in finding effective ways to reach our target audience, engage them, and ultimately convert them into happy, paying clients.

Challenge 7: Marketing

Let's be honest, marketing and sales can feel like a foreign language at times. We have a fantastic product or service, but how do we effectively communicate its value to potential customers? Crafting compelling marketing messages, navigating social media algorithms, and staying on top of the latest marketing trends can be overwhelming. And when it comes to sales, asking for the sale and overcoming objections can sometimes leave us feeling uncomfortable or uncertain. It's a learning curve that requires us to step out of our comfort zones and refine our skills.

Challenge 8: Sales

Sales is one tough cookie for a lot of entrepreneurs. It takes time, energy, and a heck of a lot of patience. It's a jungle out there with everyone trying to get a piece of the same pie. Keeping up your motivation and not letting the 'no's get to you, that's a challenge. When you're starting up, you're not just the entrepreneur; you're also the main salesperson, juggling a dozen roles, which can be tough. It's complex, needs different strategies at each step, and can be time-consuming.

Challenge 9: Support System

Having a solid support system is crucial, my friend. But sometimes, it feels like we're in this entrepreneurial journey alone. We yearn for a community of like-minded individuals who truly understand the challenges we face. It's not just about having people who cheer us on; it's about finding those who can provide guidance, advice, and a shoulder to lean on when things get tough. Building a support system can be a struggle, but it's worth the effort to find our tribe and team.

Challenge 10: Adapting change

It's funny how we entrepreneurs are. We dive headfirst into creating something new, something different. We love to innovate, to disrupt. But then, when it comes to change, especially while building our businesses, we sometimes put on the brakes. Perhaps it's the fear of the unknown, the comfort of our plans, or just the sheer pace of change that can make it tough.

Do you often find yourself stuck in one or more of these given situations?

As a fellow woman entrepreneur, I understand the unique journey you're embarking upon, filled with countless possibilities, growth, and, of course, challenges. While challenges may seem daunting, they are not roadblocks on your path to success; they are stepping stones that will elevate you to new heights. Each obstacle presents an opportunity for growth, learning, and self-discovery. It's in these moments of struggle that we find our greatest strengths, resilience, and ingenuity.

I want to emphasize the importance of paying attention to the challenges a woman encounters along the way, as they hold the key to unlocking your true potential and achieving unparalleled success.

By recognizing and addressing these challenges head-on, you empower yourself to navigate the often-turbulent waters of entrepreneurship with grace and confidence.

Moreover, understanding and overcoming these challenges will position you as a role model and inspiration for future generations of women entrepreneurs.

My fellow woman entrepreneur, I invite you to embrace the challenges that lie ahead. Approach them with an open mind, a courageous spirit, and an unwavering belief in your own abilities.

This book will offer practical strategies to overcome specific challenges faced by women in business and life. I will provide you with a toolkit of knowledge, insights, and actionable steps to help you navigate the complexities of entrepreneurship while preserving your well-being and personal life.

CHAPTER 2

SELF DISCOVERY

I vividly remember the day I met Riddhi, the owner of a beautiful jewelry store. Her store had been in business for five years, and she had poured her heart and soul into creating exquisite pieces of jewelers. But despite her initial success, she had hit a roadblock in the past two years. Her business seemed to be stagnating, and she couldn't figure out how to break through the barrier that was holding her back.

As we sat down together, sipping our coffees, Riddhi expressed her deep desire to become the number one jewelry store in her field. She spoke with a mix of frustration and determination, sharing how she had envisioned her business thriving and flourishing. She had dreamed of her jewelry being worn by women from all corners of the world, symbolizing elegance, and beauty.

"I started this journey with so much passion and excitement," Riddhi confided in me. "In the beginning, things were going well. I was getting recognition for my unique designs, and customers were drawn to the beauty and craftsmanship of my jewelry. But somewhere along the way, I hit a wall. I feel stuck, and it's disheartening."

As she spoke, I could feel the intensity of her desire to see her business soar to new heights. Riddhi wanted to stand out from the competition, to be known as the go-to place for exquisite jewelry.

But it wasn't just about the business for Riddhi. She desired a harmonious and fulfilling family life as well. She dreamed of having more time to spend with her loved ones, to create precious memories and cherish the simple joys of life. She wanted to strike a balance between her business ambitions and her personal relationships.

Her desires were clear - she wanted her business to experience exponential growth, to increase her revenue and profitability. gaining recognition and becoming a go-to destination for customers seeking exquisite jewelry.

But she also wanted the freedom and flexibility to nurture her personal life and create a strong foundation of love and happiness within her family. She wants to feel a sense of purpose and satisfaction in her work, while also finding joy and contentment in her personal relationships.

As I listened to Riddhi's story, I couldn't help but be captivated by her determination and unwavering spirit. Her desires resonated with me, as I had seen countless other women entrepreneurs yearning for the same things.

With a renewed sense of purpose, I assured Riddhi that she wasn't alone in her journey. Together, we would explore strategies and solutions to overcome the challenges she faced. We would work towards unlocking her business's full potential, while also helping her create a fulfilling personal life.

And so, the journey began. Riddhi and I embarked on a path of discovery and growth, with the shared belief that she could achieve her desires of business success and a harmonious family life. Little did we know that this journey would not only transform her business but also inspire and empower other women entrepreneurs along the way.

CHAPTER 3

THE PATH AHEAD

Welcome, fearless and ambitious women entrepreneurs! Get ready for a transformative journey that will revolutionize your business and propel you towards incredible growth. This adventure is all about unleashing your inner powerhouse and reaching new heights of success.

The book is further divided into four parts. Each part is made up of chapters which include strategies, key takeaways, and action steps to follow.

PART 1 - UNLOCK YOUR TRUE POTENTIAL

The first step towards unlocking your true potential is embarking on a journey of self-discovery. Take the time to understand your passions, values, and strengths. Reflect upon your personal and professional experiences and identify the areas where you shine brightest. It's time to challenge those self-limiting beliefs and break free from the constraints they impose. Embrace challenges as opportunities for growth, view failures as steppingstones to success, and seek out continuous learning and development. Embrace your strengths and celebrate your achievements. Surround yourself with a support system that uplifts and encourages you. Remember, setbacks and obstacles are part of the journey, but they do not define you. They provide opportunities to learn, grow, and bounce back stronger.

PART 2 - STEP INTO THE SPOTLIGHT

In a world brimming with opportunities and limitless potential, it's time for women entrepreneurs to step into the spotlight and harness the power of visibility. Visibility is not just about being seen; it's about making a lasting impact and leaving an indelible mark on your industry. It's about positioning yourself as a go-to expert, a thought leader, and a trusted authority. By showcasing your expertise and sharing your unique voice, you attract the attention and admiration of your ideal clients, partners, and collaborators. Your visibility becomes a magnet that draws opportunities, clients, and collaborations effortlessly towards you. It's time to enhance your visibility and make your presence known in the market. Through strategic branding, captivating content, and powerful online presence, you'll become a magnet for your target audience. The world is waiting to recognize and appreciate the incredible value you bring. Get ready to step into the spotlight!

PART 3 - BUILD YOUR CREDIBILITY

Becoming a respected authority in your industry is the key to unlocking new doors of opportunity. Picture yourself as the go-to expert, commanding respect, and admiration from your peers. By sharing your knowledge, showcasing your expertise, and establishing thought leadership, you'll rise above the competition and solidify your position as a trusted leader. Building your authority takes time and dedication. It's about consistently showcasing your expertise, providing value to your audience, and demonstrating your commitment to excellence.

PART 4 - BUILD A STRONG SUPPORT SYSTEM

Entrepreneurship can be a lonely journey, but not anymore. Imagine surrounding yourself with a supportive tribe of like-minded individuals who inspire, uplift, and collaborate with you. Together, you'll celebrate successes, navigate challenges, and create an unstoppable force. Building a thriving tribe also encourages personal and professional growth. Engaging with individuals who are on a similar path can push you to step out of your comfort zone, challenge yourself, and continuously strive for improvement. By being part of a tribe that values growth and development, you'll be inspired to reach new heights of success.

Throughout this book, we'll deep dive into each step, providing you with invaluable insights, practical strategies, key learnings, and actions to take. So, buckle up, gather your determination, and let's dive into the world of exponential business growth like never before!

Part 2

UNLEASH YOUR INNER POTENTIAL

CHAPTER 4

THE MINDSET MAGIC

"We are what our thoughts have made us; so, take care about what you think. Words are secondary. Thoughts live; they travel far."

- Swami Vivekananda

In Pune's tech hub, Kalyani had established her software startup. With years of expertise, she knew she had a product that could revolutionize online education.

Kalyani believed in her traditional ways. "This is how we've always done it," was her motto. While her peers constantly adapted to new technologies and methodologies, Kalyani hesitated. She feared failures, rejections, and the uncertainty of the future. Any suggestion for change was met with skepticism. Her business began to suffer. Competitors, who were more adaptable, started gaining more traction, while Kalyani's company stagnated. Revenues dropped, clients moved on, and her team became demotivated.

One day, her friend Anusha, an entrepreneur herself, visited. Seeing the situation, she advised, "Kalyani, change isn't the enemy. Fear is." Anusha introduced her to growth mindset workshops. Reluctantly, Kalyani attended one. The stories of failures leading to success, and the value of adaptability, resonated with her. It wasn't an overnight transformation, but Kalyani slowly started embracing change.

A year later, with a revamped product and a renewed spirit, her company began its ascent once more. Kalyani had learned that growth often comes from letting go of old certainties.

Kalyani's story is a testament to the power of mindset. Her journey wasn't easy, but it was possible, thanks to the shift in her mindset. It underlines the truth that, as women entrepreneurs, your skills, passion, and vision is essential. Still, without the right mindset, these tools remain underutilized.

In the quest for business growth, one of the most crucial factors that can determine your success is your mindset. A growth mindset is not just a buzzword; it is a transformative way of thinking that opens a world of possibilities. Without the right mindset, even the most brilliant strategies and opportunities can go to waste.

Mindset plays a pivotal role in achieving business growth. It shapes our thoughts, beliefs, and actions, ultimately determining our level of success. Cultivating a powerful mindset is not always easy. It requires dedication, persistence, and a commitment to personal growth. But remember, you are capable of far more than you can imagine.

STRATEGY

Believe in Yourself:

You have unique talents, skills, and experiences that set you apart. Embrace your strengths and believe in your ability to succeed. Trust in yourself and your capabilities, for self-belief is the foundation of a powerful mindset.

Embrace Growth:

Successful entrepreneurs understand that there is always something new to learn and room for growth. They eagerly seek out knowledge and skills, constantly honing their craft and staying abreast of industry trends. Embrace the concept of continuous learning and improvement. Every setback, challenge, and failure is an opportunity for growth. Embrace them with open arms, for they are stepping stones to your ultimate success.

Practice Resilience:

Entrepreneurship is a journey filled with ups and downs. Embrace resilience as your companion, and view setbacks as temporary roadblocks rather than permanent barriers. Develop the ability to bounce back from challenges and keep moving forward.

Stay Curious:

Maintain a sense of curiosity and an openness to new ideas and perspectives. Embrace a mindset of exploration and innovation, as it is through curiosity that you discover new opportunities and push the boundaries of what is possible.

Focus on solutions:

A solution-oriented mindset is also fundamental to developing a growth mindset. Rather than dwelling on problems, successful entrepreneurs focus on finding solutions. They approach obstacles as puzzles to be solved and tap into their creativity and resourcefulness to overcome them.

Positive attitude:

Another crucial aspect of a growth mindset is fostering a positive attitude towards challenges and setbacks. Rather than seeing them as roadblocks, successful entrepreneurs view them as steppingstones to success. They understand that challenges offer valuable opportunities for growth and improvement. You reinforce positive beliefs about your abilities and potential for success, which directly impacts your motivation, decision-making, and overall mindset.

Practice gratitude:

Gratitude involves acknowledging and appreciating the positive aspects of your life, including both big and small things. When you cultivate gratitude, you shift your focus from what is lacking or challenging to what you have and what is going well. This shift in perspective allows you to develop a positive outlook on life and business. It reminds you of your strengths, accomplishments, and the resources available to you, boosting your confidence and resilience.

Seek support:

Surrounding ourselves with like-minded individuals who inspire and uplift us can make a significant difference in our mindset and overall success. We can seek out mentors, join mastermind groups, or connect with a community of entrepreneurs who share our goals and aspirations.

KEY LEARNINGS

- A positive mindset is a powerful catalyst for success and growth.
- Believing in yourself and your abilities is crucial for achieving your goals.
- Resilience and optimism fuel perseverance in the face of challenges.
- Embracing a growth mindset opens doors to endless possibilities and learning opportunities.
- Cultivating habit of gratitude and practicing positive self-talk trains your mind to focus on abundance and positivity rather than dwelling on negatives.

ACTIONS

- Every morning or night, jot down three things you're grateful for. They don't have to be big–sometimes the smallest joys make the most impact.
- Dedicate at least 15 minutes daily to learn something new, whether it's reading an article, watching a tutorial, or practicing a new skill.
- Spend 10 minutes each day practicing mindfulness or meditation. Focus on your breathing, sensations, or positive affirmations during this time.

CHAPTER 5

BELIEFS UNLEASHED

"Believe in yourself and all that you are. Know that there is something inside you that is greater than any obstacle."

- Christian D. Larson

Our beliefs have a remarkable influence on how we perceive ourselves, others, and the world around us. They act as filters through which we interpret experiences, make decisions, and navigate our lives. Beliefs can either empower us to achieve greatness or hold us back from reaching our full potential. Understanding the power of beliefs is the first step in realizing the immense impact they have on our personal and professional growth.

Limiting beliefs impact our personal and professional growth. They are those deeply ingrained thoughts and perceptions that restrict us from pursuing our dreams and goals. They often stem from past experiences, societal conditioning, or negative self-talk. These beliefs create self-imposed limitations, preventing us from taking risks, stepping out of our comfort zones, and embracing new opportunities.

By recognizing the influence of beliefs, questioning their validity, and adopting empowering perspectives, we can create a shift in mindset that propels us towards personal and professional success. As we navigate through the process of self-discovery and growth, remember that you have the power to shape your reality and transform your life.

To begin our transformative journey, we must first identify the self-limiting beliefs that may be lurking in the shadows of our minds. These beliefs can manifest as thoughts like "I'm not good enough," "I don't deserve success," or "I'm afraid of failure." By shining a light on these beliefs, we can bring them to the forefront and challenge their validity. It's time to challenge the beliefs that have been holding you back and step into a future filled with boundless opportunities.

STRATEGY

Self-confidence:

This is the armor that shields us from the doubts and criticisms that may come our way. When you have a strong belief in yourself and your abilities, you develop the courage and resilience to confront those self-imposed limitations and a recognition of our worth. You possess within you a reservoir of strength, resilience, and untapped potential. You are worthy of success, happiness, and fulfillment in both your personal and professional life.

Self-awareness:

To challenge and overcome limiting beliefs, it's essential to become aware of our self-perception and self-talk patterns. By recognizing how we perceive ourselves and the language we use internally, we can identify the negative narratives that contribute to our limiting beliefs. Once we become conscious of these patterns, we can begin to reframe our self-perception and transform our self-talk.

Self -compassion:

As women entrepreneurs, we often set high expectations for ourselves and can be overly critical when we fall short. Cultivating self-compassion allows us to acknowledge our mistakes and imperfections without judgment, offering ourselves the same understanding and support we would give to a close friend. It involves practicing self-care, self-validation, and embracing our humanity. By cultivating self-compassion, we develop resilience, bounce back from setbacks, and foster a positive and empowering mindset.

Growth mindset:

Shifting from a fixed mindset to a growth mindset is essential for the growth and success of women business owners. By embracing a growth mindset, you believe that challenges are opportunities for growth, setbacks are steppingstones to success, and effort leads to mastery. Replacing statements by adding yet, "I can't do this" with "I can't do this yet," acknowledges that skills and abilities can be developed over time with effort and practice. This mindset empowers you to embrace continuous learning, take on new challenges, and persist in the face of obstacles.

Affirmations:

Positive affirmations are powerful statements that reflect the beliefs, qualities, and outcomes we want to manifest. By repeating them regularly, we reprogram our subconscious mind and reinforce empowering beliefs. For example, as a woman entrepreneur, you might create affirmations like "I am confident in my abilities to grow my business," "I attract abundant opportunities and clients," or "I am worthy of success and fulfillment." Visualizing these affirmations in vivid detail strengthens the neural pathways associated with these beliefs, making them more ingrained in our mindset.

Visualisation:

Visualization involves creating vivid mental images of yourself already achieving your goals and experiencing success. By visualizing your desired outcomes, you stimulate your imagination and subconscious mind to align with those empowering beliefs. Feel the emotions associated with those accomplishments as if they are already a reality. Visualization helps to solidify empowering beliefs and enhances your motivation, focus, and determination.

Embrace uncertainty:

Growth and transformation happen outside of our comfort zones. To achieve exponential growth in our businesses, we must be willing to embrace uncertainty, take calculated risks, and explore uncharted territories. Stepping outside of our comfort zones means challenging the familiar and venturing into the unknown. It requires courage, resilience, and a willingness to learn and adapt along the way.

Celebrate small victories:

Celebrating small victories along the way is essential for maintaining momentum and staying motivated on our journey towards exponential business growth. By acknowledging and celebrating even the smallest wins, we build confidence, reinforce positive habits, and cultivate a success-oriented mindset. These small victories create a snowball effect, propelling us forward with increased momentum and propelling us towards our larger goals.

Trust in your abilities:

Trusting in your abilities allows you to silence the self-doubt and negative self-talk that may creep in during challenging times. It enables you to reframe setbacks and failures as opportunities for growth and learning. Rather than dwelling on past mistakes, you maintain a forward-thinking mindset, seeking solutions and lessons that will contribute to your future success.

Take that leap of faith and watch as you soar to new heights you never thought. Remember that the only limits that exist are the ones you impose upon yourself. Break free from the chains of self-doubt and embrace the boundless possibilities that await you. You have the power to shape your destiny and create a future filled with abundance, success, and fulfillment.

KEY LEARNINGS

- Self-awareness is the first step in identifying and challenging limiting beliefs that hold you back.
- By questioning the validity of your limiting beliefs, you can create new empowering beliefs.
- Stepping out of your comfort zone and taking calculated risks helps challenge and overcome limiting beliefs.
- Maintain a forward-thinking mindset for future success.

- Surrounding yourself with supportive and positive influences can reinforce your belief in what's possible.

ACTIONS

- Begin your day by repeating positive affirmations about your abilities.
- Engage daily with positive and motivating content, whether it's a motivational podcast, an inspiring book, or conversing with uplifting friends or mentors.
- At the end of each day, list three things you've achieved, no matter how small. Celebrate once they are accomplished.
- Replace “I can’t, with a resounding affirmation: "I can, and I will!"

CHAPTER 6

POWER TO SHAPE OUTCOMES

"When you think everything is someone else's fault, you will suffer a lot. When you realize that everything springs only from yourself, you will learn both peace and joy."

- Dalai Lama

Asha was a talented artist living in Ahmedabad with a passion for creating one-of-a-kind pieces of jewelry. Asha often blamed her situation for not following her dreams. She would say, "If I didn't have this job, I would start my own business," or "If I had more support, I could have been an entrepreneur." This way, she kept deflecting responsibility onto circumstances, never fully owning her life.

One day, Asha met Sunita who was an entrepreneur who had started her own successful clothing line from scratch. Sunita shared her journey, highlighting the successes and failures she had encountered. Asha couldn't help but notice one quality - Sunita never shied away from taking responsibility for her life, she owned all her decisions, successes, and failures alike. It was evident that taking complete responsibility for her life was a critical part of her success.

Inspired by Sunita's story, Asha began reflecting on her own life. She realized that by blaming her circumstances, she was giving away her power to change them. decided to take complete responsibility for her life, understanding that the first step to change was in her hands.

Asha's story is a powerful reminder to every woman entrepreneur about the importance of taking complete responsibility for one's life. It's easy to blame circumstances or other people when things go wrong. But true power lies in acknowledging that we are the architects of our lives.

In the journey of entrepreneurship, one of the most empowering decisions you can make is to take full responsibility for your actions and results. Taking ownership of your choices and outcomes means recognizing that the decisions you make have a direct impact on the trajectory of your business.

Taking responsibility for your actions and results is a transformative mindset that empowers you to take control of your journey as a woman entrepreneur. Embrace this responsibility with confidence, determination, and resilience, and watch as your business thrives and surpasses your wildest dreams.

STRATEGY

It Starts with You:

You are the driving force behind your success. The moment you fully embrace this truth, you reclaim your power and become the catalyst for change. Your commitment to personal growth and responsibility will inspire others and attract the right opportunities and collaborations.

Empower Yourself:

By taking 100% responsibility, you empower yourself to transcend limitations and break through barriers. Only you have the power to transform challenges into opportunities and setbacks into steppingstones towards success. It means understanding that you have the power to shape the outcomes of your business and taking the necessary steps to navigate challenges and seize opportunities.

Become proactive:

When you embrace a proactive mindset, you become proactive rather than reactive in your approach to your business. Instead of waiting for things to happen or relying on external factors, you take initiative and actively seek out opportunities. You are constantly on the lookout for ways to improve, grow, and innovate.

Take accountability:

Accountability goes hand in hand with being proactive. It means taking ownership of your choices, actions, and outcomes. You understand that the success or failure of your business ultimately rests on your shoulders. You recognize that success is not a result of luck or circumstances, but a result of your intentional actions and decisions.

Learn from Failures:

Failure is not the end; it is a steppingstone to success. When you take responsibility for your results, you view failures as valuable lessons rather than roadblocks. Embrace failures as opportunities to learn, adapt, and grow stronger.

Lead by Example:

As a responsible entrepreneur, you become a role model for others. Your commitment to taking responsibility sets the tone for your team, clients, and business partners. By leading by example, you create a culture of accountability and excellence.

By taking 100% responsibility for your actions and results, you become the master of your own destiny and create a path to success that is driven by your choices and efforts. However, taking 100% responsibility is not always easy. It requires courage, self-reflection, and a willingness to step outside your comfort zone. But the rewards are immeasurable.

So, as you continue your entrepreneurial journey, let the flame of responsibility burn bright within you. You have the power. You have the ability. Take 100% responsibility and write your own success story. The world is waiting for you to shine.

KEY LEARNINGS

- Taking ownership of your choices and actions empowers you to shape your business's outcomes.
- Embracing a proactive and accountable mindset allows you to navigate challenges and seize opportunities.
- Recognizing that you are in control of your business growth empowers you to make impactful decisions.
- Embracing responsibility fosters a sense of empowerment and control over your own success.
- Accepting responsibility for your actions allows you to learn from mistakes and grow as a business owner.

ACTIONS

- Dedicate 10 minutes at the end of the day to reflect on what went well, where you faced challenges, and what lessons you learned. Document these reflections.

CHAPTER 7

CHARTING YOUR PATH TO SUCCESS

"The only thing standing between you and your goal is the story you keep telling yourself as to why you can't achieve it."

-Jordan Belfort

Goals give us direction, facilitate decision-making, and motivate us to act. They allow us to measure our progress and celebrate our victories, however small they may be.

There is a lot written on goal setting by the experts in the industry, however let me give 5 top reasons why as a woman entrepreneur you should have your goals in place.

Reason no 1

One of the key benefits of goal setting is that it provides focus, and we create a clear vision of where we want to go and what we want to achieve with a clear focus, you can avoid getting side-tracked by distractions and stay on track towards your desired outcomes. It helps you prioritize your actions, make informed decisions, stay focused on what truly matters and allocate your time, energy, and resources towards activities that align with your objectives. Goals serve as a powerful tool that not only directs our actions but also shapes our mindset and attitude.

Reason no 2

Goals encourage you to think big and aim high. By setting ambitious yet attainable goals, you push yourself beyond your comfort zone and challenge your own capabilities. This mindset shift opens doors to new possibilities and fosters personal and professional growth.

Reason no 3

Setting specific and measurable goals allows you to track your progress and evaluate your performance. It enables you to gauge how far you have come and identify areas where you need to adjust or improve. This feedback loop helps you stay accountable to yourself and make informed decisions along the way.

Reason no 4

Goals also serve as a powerful source of motivation. When you have a compelling vision of what you want to achieve, it ignites a fire within you and fuels your drive to take consistent action. Goals act as a constant reminder of why you started your business in the first place and the aspirations you have for its growth and success.

Reason no 5

Goals allow us to seize opportunities that come our way. When we have a clear vision of what we want to achieve, we become more attuned to recognizing opportunities that align with our goals. We become more proactive in seeking out connections, resources, and experiences that can support our progress.

STRATEGY

Craft a compelling vision statement

Your vision statement is a powerful declaration that paints a vivid picture of what you aspire your business to become in the future. It should inspire and motivate both you and your team, serving as a guiding star for your business. For example, a vision statement for a sustainable fashion brand could be,

"To create a world where ethical and eco-friendly fashion is the norm, empowering individuals to make conscious and stylish choices."

Develop a mission statement.

Your mission statement defines the purpose and identity of your business. It communicates the value you provide to your customers, the principles you uphold, and what makes your business unique. A mission statement for a digital marketing agency could be, "To help 1000 small businesses thrive in the digital landscape by delivering innovative and results-driven marketing solutions that generate meaningful connections and sustainable growth."

Create an action plan

Create an action plan is to break down your goals into smaller, manageable tasks. By breaking them down into bite-sized actions, you can tackle them one at a time, making the overall goal less overwhelming. Each task should be specific, measurable, achievable, relevant, and time-bound (SMART). This ensures that they are clear, quantifiable, realistic, and aligned with your larger goal.

Set milestones and deadlines:

It is crucial to establish key milestones and deadlines. Break down your action plan into smaller time frames, such as weekly or monthly targets, and monitor your progress regularly. These are milestones that will help you track your progress and provides a sense of accomplishment as you reach

each milestone. Deadlines create a sense of urgency and ensure that you stay on track and make consistent progress towards your goal.

Develop strategies to overcome roadblocks:

It's important to identify potential challenges and obstacles that may arise along the way. These can include resource limitations, market competition, technological advancements, or personal limitations. By being proactive and acknowledging these potential hurdles, you can develop contingency plans and prepare yourself mentally to face them head-on.

Track and evaluate progress:

It allows you to monitor your advancement, identify areas of improvement, and make informed decisions to stay on track. These can include revenue growth, customer acquisition rates, website traffic, social media engagement, or any other measurable parameters relevant to your business.

The key to success lies in taking consistent action and staying committed to your plan. So, take that first step, create your action plan, and let it guide you towards the realization of your goals.

By embracing the power of goal setting, you have laid the foundation for your future success and exponential growth.

As you move forward, stay focused on your goals, remain adaptable in the face of change, and celebrate every milestone along the way. Remember that success is not just a destination; it is a continuous journey of growth and self-discovery.

KEY LEARNINGS

- Setting clear and specific goals gives you direction and purpose in your business.
- Aligning your goals with your values and vision creates a sense of meaning and fulfillment.
- Breaking down big goals into smaller, actionable steps makes them more attainable and manageable.
- Regularly reviewing and adjusting your goals helps you stay on track and adapt to changing circumstances.
- Celebrating milestones and achievements along the way keeps you motivated and inspired to continue striving for success.

ACTIONS

- Write main monthly/quarterly goals prominently in your workspace.
- Each day, select a smaller segment of that goal that you can realistically tackle.
- List tasks needed to accomplish the daily segment of your goal.
- Allocate specific blocks of uninterrupted time to each task.
- Before bed, take a moment to visualize achieving your broader goals.

Part 3

CARVE YOUR VISIBILITY

CHAPTER 8

FIND YOUR NICHE

"Don't find customers for your products, find products for your customers."

- Seth Godin

Sunita always dreamed of running her own clothing boutique in the bustling heart of Mumbai. Driven by passion, she poured her savings into Sunita's Saree Saga, expecting the city's women to flock to her unique designs. However, months passed, and the shop remained quiet. Desperation grew as bills piled up.

Her friend, Aarti, noticed Sunita's stress during their chai catch-up. "Who exactly are your sarees for, Sunita?" she asked gently. Sunita's designs varied wildly, from college-friendly styles to luxurious wedding wear. Realization hit; she was trying to please everyone and connecting with no one.

With Aarti's encouragement, Sunita decided to focus on what she loved most - elegant, traditional sarees. She rebranded, restocked, and reached out to local communities celebrating traditional wear. Slowly, word spread, and women began seeking out her unique collection. Sunita's business wasn't just a shop anymore; it was a destination for tradition.

Finding your niche is like discovering a hidden treasure within the vast business landscape. It involves identifying a specific target market that aligns with your expertise, interests, and the unique value you bring to the table. By honing on a niche, you position yourself as a specialist, allowing you to deeply understand your audience and cater to their distinct needs. It's a powerful strategy that leads to stronger customer relationships, increased brand loyalty, and ultimately, business growth.

While numerous experts offer a variety of perspectives on this topic, I'd like to highlight my personal rationale for emphasizing the importance of a niche.

Stand out in a crowded market:

In today's highly competitive business landscape, finding your niche allows you to differentiate yourself from the competition. By targeting a specific segment of the market, you can focus your resources, expertise, and messaging, making it easier for potential customers to recognize and choose your business. It helps you cut through the noise and establish a unique position that sets you apart as a go-to expert in your field.

Understand and cater to your ideal customers:

When you identify a niche, you gain a deep understanding of your target audience's specific needs, pain points, and desires. This knowledge enables you to develop tailored products or services that truly address their challenges and aspirations. By catering to a niche market, you can create a more personalized and impactful customer experience, fostering strong connections and building a loyal customer base.

Increase brand credibility and expertise:

By focusing on a specific niche, you position yourself as an authority and specialist in that area. This specialization enhances your brand's credibility and perceived expertise, making it easier for potential customers to trust and rely on your offerings. As a woman business owner, showcasing your expertise in a niche market can also help overcome any gender biases that might exist within your industry, solidifying your position as a leader.

Enhance marketing effectiveness:

With a well-defined niche, your marketing efforts become more targeted and effective. You can tailor your messaging, branding, and communication channels to resonate specifically with your ideal customers. This ensures that your marketing campaigns reach the right people at the right time, increasing the chances of engagement and conversion. It also enables you to allocate your marketing budget more efficiently, focusing on platforms and strategies that align with your niche audience.

Command premium pricing:

When you specialize in a niche, you can position your products or services as unique and valuable, allowing you to command premium pricing. By clearly articulating the benefits and value you offer through your USP, customers are willing to pay a premium for a specialized solution that meets their specific needs. This contributes to increased profitability and helps you build a sustainable and thriving business.

STRATEGY

Research Your Market:

Conducting market research to identify potential niches. It involves gathering information about your target market, industry trends, and customer preferences. By conducting thorough market research, you can uncover opportunities and uncover untapped niche markets.

Assess your market:

Assessing market demand involves analyzing the size of the target market, identifying the pain points or unmet needs of potential customers, and understanding their purchasing behavior. This information helps you gauge the market's appetite for products or services in your niche.

Evaluate the market:

Once you have identified potential niches, it is important to evaluate their market demand, competition, and trends. This evaluation ensures that you choose a niche that is viable and has the potential for business growth. Understanding their strengths, weaknesses, pricing strategies, and unique selling points can help you identify gaps or areas where you can differentiate yourself.

Study customer needs and pain points:

Understand the specific problems or desires of your target audience within each niche. Look for gaps or underserved areas that your business can address.

Monitor industry trends:

Stay updated on industry news, technological advancements, and changing consumer preferences to identify emerging trends that could shape your chosen niches.

Conduct customer surveys:

Interviews and online research to gather insights allows you to gather first-hand information about their needs, preferences, and pain points. This information will guide your decision-making process as you narrow down your niche options and develop a strong value proposition that resonates with your customers.

Assess Your Skills, Passion, and Expertise

Identifying your unique strengths, skills, and expertise. Make a list of the specific skills you have acquired through education, training, or work experience. Identify your areas of expertise and the areas where you excel. Consider your personal qualities, such as leadership, problem-solving, creativity, or adaptability.

Evaluate your passions and interests that align with potential niches

Consider the activities, subjects, or causes that genuinely ignite your enthusiasm. Reflect on what brings you joy and fulfillment, as this will contribute to your motivation and long-term commitment in your business. Explore areas of personal interest that can align with potential niches. Look for connections between your passions and the needs or desires of your target market. Finding a niche that aligns with your interests will make your work more enjoyable and fulfilling.

Identify gaps in the market:

Look for areas within your industry where there may be underserved customer needs or unexplored opportunities. Assess how your skills and passion can help fill these gaps.

Consider the viability and scalability:

Assess the long-term potential of a niche by evaluating the market size, competition, and potential for business growth. Determine if there is a sustainable market for your products or services that aligns with your expertise and passion.

By harnessing the power of finding your niche you can transform your business from being just another player in the market to becoming a distinctive, sought-after brand.

KEY LEARNINGS

- Identifying your target audience and understanding their needs helps you tailor your products or services for maximum impact.
- Differentiating yourself from competitors by focusing on a specific niche allows you to stand out and attract loyal customers.
- Researching market trends and consumer demands helps you uncover untapped opportunities within your chosen niche.
- Aligning your passion and expertise with your niche enhances your authenticity and connection with your target audience.
- Continuously evaluating and adapting your niche strategy ensures long-term relevance and growth in your business.

ACTIONS

- List down your passions, interests, and strengths.
- Join industry-specific groups, forums, or associations related to your niche.
- Connect with potential customers.
- Lookout for courses, books, or webinars relevant to your niche.

CHAPTER 9

CRAFT A UNIQUE SELLING POINT

"In order to be irreplaceable, one must always be different."

- Coco Chanel

In Goa, there lived an energetic woman named Era who had a deep love for surfing and a keen sense of business. She dreamt of merging her passion and skill by starting a surfboard shop. With unwavering determination, Era opened her store, 'Surf's Up,' offering a range of surfboards.

Despite her passion, knowledge, and quality products, Era found herself struggling to compete with other established surf shops in town. Even though she knew her surfboards were of excellent quality, she couldn't convince enough customers to choose 'Surf's Up' over other stores. Disheartened yet determined, Emma sought advice.

She met Hema, a successful entrepreneur known for her unique candle business. Hema had created a successful brand by selling candles that replicated the scents of different locations, a truly unique selling proposition. Intrigued, Era asked Hema how she differentiated her products in such a saturated market.

Hema shared her business story, explaining, "In a competitive market, having a quality product isn't enough. You need a unique selling proposition - something that sets you apart from everyone else."

This conversation sparked an idea in Era's mind. She knew her shop couldn't just be another surfboard retailer; it had to offer something special. Era thought about what she loved about surfing. It was not just the sport itself, but also the connection with the ocean, the feel of the water, the beauty of the early morning waves. This connection with nature was what made surfing special for Era.

Era decided to carve out a unique selling point for 'Surf's Up'. She started crafting eco-friendly surfboards, made with sustainable materials and processes, promoting a closer connection with nature. Her surfboards were not just sports equipment but a statement of love and respect for the ocean.

Era's story highlights the power of a unique selling point in a competitive business environment. It shows how a unique selling point can help a business stand out, attract a loyal customer base, and create a strong brand identity.

As a woman business owner, you possess the drive and determination to make your mark in the business world. A power of crafting a USP is that it will set your business apart from the competition. A well-crafted USP is a vital tool for attracting customers, driving growth, and achieving exponential success.

The significance of a USP in differentiating your business and attracting customers. It is the key to differentiation. It is a concise and compelling statement that communicates the unique value and benefits your business offers to customers. A strong USP creates a distinct identity for your brand, making it memorable and compelling in the minds of your target audience. By clearly articulating what sets your business apart, you attract customers who are seeking precisely what you offer.

For women-owned businesses, a well-crafted USP is particularly crucial. It allows you to break through gender biases and establish your presence in your industry. A strong USP highlights your unique perspective, expertise, and values, making a powerful statement in the market. By effectively communicating your USP, you can attract a loyal customer base, build credibility, and accelerate the growth of your business. A compelling USP empowers women entrepreneurs to make their mark and achieve exponential growth and success.

The key components of a strong USP: uniqueness, value, and differentiation

Uniqueness:

Your USP should highlight what sets your business apart from competitors. It could be a unique feature, a proprietary technology, exceptional customer service, or a distinctive brand personality. By emphasizing your unique qualities, you create a memorable and distinct impression in the minds of customers.

Value:

Your USP should clearly communicate the value and benefits customers will receive by choosing your products or services. It should address their pain points, desires, or aspirations and demonstrate how your offerings provide a solution or fulfill their needs better than alternatives in the market. By showcasing the value, you deliver, you create a compelling reason for customers to choose you.

Differentiation:

Your USP should highlight how you differentiate yourself from competitors. It could be through superior quality, a unique approach, competitive pricing, or a specialized niche focus. By clearly communicating what makes you different, you establish a competitive advantage that positions you as the preferred choice for your target audience.

STRATEGY

Identify Your Business's Unique Qualities and Value Proposition:

Understand what sets your business apart from competitors and identify areas where you excel. Clearly communicate and highlight the value and benefits that set you apart and position you as the preferred choice.

Take stock of your business's strengths, whether it's specialized knowledge, exceptional customer service, innovative technology, or unique resources. Determine what advantages your business has over competitors. This could be factors such as lower costs, faster delivery, higher quality, or a more comprehensive range of products or services.

Assess how these advantages can benefit your target customers and contribute to your unique value proposition. Consider the unique qualities that define your business's identity and brand. This could be your company culture, values, or a compelling origin story. Identify aspects that resonate with your target audience and differentiate you in the market.

Understand the needs, desires, and pain points of your target customers:

Use market research techniques to gain insights into the needs, desires, and pain points of your target customers. Understand their motivations, challenges, and aspirations related to the products or services you offer. Engage in conversations with your existing customers to understand their experiences, preferences, and expectations. Identify any gaps or unaddressed pain points that you can capitalize on to provide unique solutions.

Find the intersection between your unique qualities and customer needs:

Evaluate the unique qualities and strengths of your business against the needs, desires, and pain points of your target customers. Based on the alignment identified, craft a clear and compelling value proposition that communicates the specific benefits customers will receive by choosing your products or services. Highlight the unique aspects of your business that differentiate you in the market. Communicate how these unique qualities contribute to the value you offer and why customers should choose you over alternatives.

Leverage Your USP for Growth and Success:

Integrate your USP across all marketing channels and touchpoints. Ensure that your USP is communicated consistently across all marketing channels. Develop targeted marketing campaigns that focus on the specific pain points or desires addressed by your USP. This consistency builds brand recognition and reinforces your unique value proposition. Use your USP as the foundation for your brand's storytelling. Engage your audience emotionally by sharing stories that resonate with their values and aspirations. Incorporate your USP visually through design elements, colors, imagery, and branding. These visual cues should evoke the essence of your unique value proposition, reinforcing it in the minds of your target customers.

Leverage the power of social proof by featuring customer testimonials and success stories that emphasize the positive outcomes achieved through your unique value proposition.

Evolve and adapt your USP:

Regularly conduct market research to gather insights that inform the evolution of your USP and ensure its continued relevance. Actively seek feedback from your customers to understand their evolving needs and expectations. Your USP should remain agile, allowing you to seize new opportunities, address emerging trends, and stay ahead of the competition. Continuously monitor the impact of your USP on business growth and customer engagement. By integrating your USP across all marketing channels, differentiating yourself from competitors, and evolving your USP as your business grows, you can leverage its power for sustained growth and success.

As woman entrepreneurs, empower yourself with an authentic, unique, and customer centric USP, and you can position your business for exponential growth and success. Remember, you have the power to shape your own destiny as a woman entrepreneur. Embrace your strengths, be true to yourself, and create a USP that authentically reflects who you are and what you offer. Let your USP be the catalyst that propels you forward, attracting your ideal customers and driving your business to new heights of achievement. The journey starts now, and the possibilities are limitless!

KEY LEARNINGS

- Identifying and showcasing your unique strengths, qualities, or offerings sets you apart from competitors.
- Understanding your target audience's needs and preferences helps you tailor your unique selling point to resonate with them.
- Communicating a clear and compelling value proposition establishes a strong connection with your customers.
- Consistently delivering on your unique selling point builds trust, loyalty, and brand recognition.
- Continuously evaluating and evolving your unique selling point ensures its relevance and effectiveness in the ever-changing market.
- **ACTIONS**
- List out points what makes your product or service unique.
- How does your product or service make your customers feel?
- Before finalizing your USP, test it out. Share it with a few trusted customers or peers and gather feedback.
- Once you've crafted your USP, make sure it's integrated into all your branding and marketing materials.

CHAPTER 10

BUILD A PERSONAL BRAND

"If people like you they will listen to you, but if they trust you, they'll do business with you."

- Zig Ziglar

Personal branding allows you to showcase your expertise, values, and personality, creating a strong and memorable impression. An impactful image goes beyond your professional appearance; it encompasses how you present yourself, communicate, and engage with others. When you cultivate an impactful image, you enhance your credibility, building trust and confidence in the minds of your audience. It also increases your visibility, making you more recognizable and memorable in a crowded marketplace. Furthermore, an impactful image has the power to attract opportunities. It can draw the attention of potential clients, partners, and industry influencers, opening doors to collaborations, speaking engagements, and other growth opportunities. By investing in personal branding and cultivating an impactful image, you position yourself as a standout entrepreneur in your field, setting the stage for long-term success and growth.

By being true to yourself, you attract the right audience, who will appreciate you and support your brand. In a world where trends and fads come and go, being authentic is timeless and enduring. It sets you apart and creates a unique space in the hearts and minds of your audience.

STRATEGY

Tell your brand story:

Crafting your personal brand story is a powerful tool for women entrepreneurs to connect with their audience on a deeper level and inspire them with their journey. Your story is more than just a chronological account of your experiences; it's an opportunity to share the challenges you've overcome, the lessons you've learned, and the vision that drives you. By developing a compelling narrative, you invite others into your world, allowing them to resonate with your authenticity and connect with your values. Your personal brand story becomes a source of inspiration, showing others that they too can overcome obstacles and achieve their goals. It creates a bond with your audience, fostering trust and loyalty.

Compelling brand message:

Your brand story is the heart and soul of your personal brand, and it should be shared across multiple platforms and channels to reach a wider audience. Whether it's through your website, social media, networking events, or speaking engagements, each channel offers a unique opportunity to showcase your brand story. It's important to tailor your messaging and storytelling techniques to each platform, ensuring consistency while adapting to the specific nuances of each medium. By effectively communicating your brand story through various channels, you increase your visibility, create brand recognition, and foster deeper connections with your audience. It allows people to understand who you are, what you stand for, and why they should choose you.

Be consistent:

Ensuring consistency across all visual elements of your brand is crucial for creating a strong and cohesive personal brand identity. Visual elements, such as your logo, color palette, typography, and imagery, play a significant role in shaping the perception of your brand. Consistency in visual elements also enhances brand recall, making it more likely that your audience will remember and recall your brand when they need the products or services you offer. So, pay attention to every visual element of your brand and ensure they align with your brand values, personality, and target audience.

Image matters:

The importance of appearance in personal branding cannot be overstated. Your appearance is an integral part of how you present yourself to the world and plays a significant role in shaping the perception of your personal brand. When it comes to personal branding, your appearance goes beyond just how you dress, it encompasses your grooming, body language, and overall presence. Your appearance creates an immediate impression and sets the tone for how others perceive and interact with you. It communicates professionalism, confidence, and attention to detail. Dressing appropriately for different occasions and environments, practicing good grooming habits, and displaying confident body language all contribute to creating a positive and impactful first impression. Invest in your professional image, pay attention to details, and let your appearance become an integral part of your personal branding strategy.

Leveraging relationships:

By actively nurturing and fostering relationships, you can tap into a network of expertise, knowledge, and connections that can propel your personal brand forward. This includes networking at industry events, engaging in online communities, and building genuine connections through meaningful conversations. By adding value to your relationships and genuinely caring about the success of others, you can build a reputation as a trusted and collaborative partner. Invest time and effort in cultivating and nurturing relationships, both online and offline. Engage with your audience, reach out to industry peers, and seek out opportunities to collaborate and support others. Your relationships can serve as advocates and ambassadors for your brand, helping to spread your message and increase your visibility.

Online presence:

It's important to regularly monitor your online presence by conducting online searches and setting up Google Alerts to stay informed about what is being said about you. Actively managing your online reputation involves taking steps to ensure that the information available about you is accurate, positive, and aligned with your personal brand. This can include regularly updating your website and social media profiles with relevant and engaging content, responding promptly and professionally to customer reviews and feedback. Regularly engaging with your online community, sharing valuable content, and maintaining a consistent and authentic voice will contribute to a strong online reputation that supports your personal brand and business growth.

Good communication:

Communication is the lifeblood of your personal brand as a woman entrepreneur. It is the bridge that connects you with your target audience, conveying your values, expertise, and unique qualities. Through clear and compelling communication, you can establish yourself as an authority in your industry, build trust with your clients and customers, and differentiate yourself from the competition. Whether it's through your spoken words, written content, or even non-verbal cues, every interaction presents an opportunity to reinforce your personal brand. Your ability to articulate your vision, purpose, and story in a relatable and authentic manner allows others to connect with you on a deeper level, fostering loyalty and engagement. Every word you choose, every message you share, and every conversation you engage in becomes an integral part of your personal brand narrative, helping you create a lasting impression in the minds and hearts of your audience.

KEY LEARNINGS

- Your personal brand should be a true reflection of who you are, your values, and your unique qualities.
- Invest in personal development, stay agile and responsive to changes in the market, industry trends, and the evolving needs of your audience.
- Use the power of storytelling to connect with your audience on a deeper level.
- Showcase your expertise, share your knowledge, and provide value to your audience through your personal brand.
- It's not about what you say but how you say.

ACTIONS

- Regularly update your skills and knowledge. Consider seeking mentors who can guide you and provide feedback.
- Be active on platforms where your audience hangs out.
- Regularly share insights, experiences, and knowledge that showcase your expertise and personality.
- Ensure that your messaging, visuals, and voice is consistent across all platforms. This strengthens brand recognition.

Part 4

BUILD YOUR CREDIBILITY

CHAPTER 11

EXPAND YOUR AUTHORITY

"Leadership is not about titles, positions, or flowcharts. It is about one life influencing another."

-John C. Maxwell

As a woman entrepreneur, it is even more important to showcase your expertise, knowledge, and unique perspective to stand out in the crowd. Building authority not only positions you as a trusted expert in your field but also opens doors to exciting opportunities, partnerships, and client relationships. By establishing authority, you become the go-to person in your niche, the one who can provide valuable solutions and insights. Building authority as a woman entrepreneur is not only about showcasing your expertise but also about embracing your unique strengths, perspectives, and experiences. It's about breaking through societal barriers and stereotypes to carve your own path to success. To build authority, it's essential to focus on developing your expertise, building a strong personal brand, creating valuable content, engaging with your audience, and collaborating with other industry influencers.

STRATEGY

Embrace Continuous learning:

To establish authority, it's crucial to adopt a mindset of continuous learning. Make a commitment to stay updated on industry trends, new technologies, and emerging best practices. Engage in professional development opportunities such as attending workshops, webinars, and industry conferences. Dedicate time each day or week to read industry publications, listen to podcasts, and follow thought leaders in your field. By staying informed and knowledgeable, you position yourself as an expert who is well-versed in the current landscape of your field.

Become a Niche Expert:

Identify a specific area within your industry that aligns with your passion and expertise. Dive deep into that niche, researching extensively and gaining practical experience. By focusing on a niche, you'll develop a reputation for specialized knowledge and attract clients or customers seeking your expertise.

Leverage Your Unique Strengths:

Reflect on your strengths, skills, and background, and consider how they differentiate you in the marketplace. What makes you stand out? How can you apply your unique perspective to solve problems and provide value to your audience? By embracing your individuality and leveraging your strengths, you'll create a distinct personal brand that resonates with your target audience.

Seek Mentorship and Collaboration:

Learning from others who have already achieved authority in your field can accelerate your own growth. Seek out mentors or industry leaders who inspire you and are willing to share their knowledge. Together, you can support and learn from each other, collectively strengthening your authority.

Share Your Knowledge:

Establishing authority requires sharing your expertise with others. Create valuable content through blog posts, articles, videos, or podcasts that educate and inspire your target audience. Your content should offer actionable advice, strategies, and tips that your audience can implement to overcome challenges and achieve their goals.

Share your own experiences, case studies, and success stories to illustrate your expertise. By consistently delivering valuable and relevant content, you build trust with your audience and establish yourself as an authority in your field.

Thought leadership:

Thought leadership is about providing unique perspectives, insights, and solutions to industry challenges. Create high-quality, well-researched content that demonstrates your knowledge and understanding of your industry. Actively participate in conversations on social media platforms, respond to comments and messages, and encourage dialogue. Listen to your audience's needs, questions, and feedback, and provide thoughtful responses.

Leveraging opportunities:

Seek out speaking engagements at industry conferences, events, or webinars where you can address a relevant audience. Prepare engaging and informative presentations that highlight your unique insights and provide actionable takeaways for the audience. By delivering impactful speeches and presentations, you can captivate the audience, build credibility, and leave a lasting impression.

Expand your circle of influence:

Attending industry events and conferences offers valuable networking opportunities to connect with like-minded professionals, industry leaders, and potential collaborators. Engage in meaningful conversations, exchange ideas, and build relationships with individuals who can further expand your influence and open doors for collaborations. By networking effectively, you can enhance your visibility, build a strong professional network, and establish yourself as a key player in your field.

Adapting to Industry Trends:

The business landscape is constantly evolving, driven by technological advancements, market shifts, and changing customer preferences. As a business owner, it is essential to stay attuned to industry trends and adapt your expertise accordingly. Monitor market developments, analyze consumer behavior, and identify emerging opportunities within your field. Update your knowledge and skills to align with the evolving needs of your target audience. By staying adaptable and proactive in response to industry changes, you can maintain your authority and position yourself as a relevant and forward-thinking expert.

Collaborate with Other Experts:

Amplify your reach and strengthen your authority by seeking opportunities to collaborate on projects, joint ventures, or co-authoring content. By combining your expertise and resources with others, you can create powerful synergies and expand your influence. Collaborative efforts such as hosting webinars, creating joint content, or organizing industry events can attract a broader audience and position you as an influential figure in your industry. Embrace collaboration to leverage collective expertise and create win-win partnerships.

KEY LEARNINGS

- Create valuable and relevant content to position yourself as an expert in your field.
- Collaborate with complementary businesses and industry influencers to significantly expand your reach and expose your brand to new audiences.
- Identify the platforms where your audience is most active and engage with them through thoughtful and valuable content.
- Actively engage with your audience and build a community around your brand.
- Position yourself as a thought leader in your industry by consistently providing valuable and insightful content to your audience

ACTIONS

- Attend industry events, webinars, workshops, and seminars.
- Engage in online communities and forums related to your niche.
- Respond to comments and engage with followers genuinely on your social media.
- Share content that provides value to your audience and showcases your expertise.

CHAPTER 12

ENHANCE YOUR MARKETING

People don't buy what you do, they buy why you do it.

- Simon Sinek

Isha was an extraordinary artisan. Her small shop, 'Leather by Isha,' housed the finest collection of handcrafted leather goods in the city. Despite her exceptional craftsmanship, Isha's business remained largely unknown beyond the local neighborhood. Her products were exquisite, but the world was oblivious to them.

One sunny afternoon, Isha met Gita, an entrepreneur who owned a successful fashion boutique in Milan. Intrigued by Isha's creations, Gita was surprised that 'Leather by Isha' was relatively unknown.

Gita explained to Isabella, "Your products are magnificent, but people need to know they exist. You're an artist, Isha, and marketing is the gallery where you showcase your art."

Pondering upon Gita's words, Isha realized that she had neglected the crucial aspect of marketing her business. She was excellent in her craft, but her craftsmanship needed visibility. Through strategic marketing, Isha transformed 'Leather by Isha' from a small local shop to a globally recognized brand.

Isha's journey underscores the importance of marketing for business growth.

Marketing is a powerful tool, indispensable for the success and growth of your business. It is the bridge that connects your products or services to the customers. Without marketing, even the best products can get lost in the market's noise.

As an entrepreneur, you might have the passion, the talent, and a great product or service. But without strategic marketing, reaching the right audience and making your business profitable can be an uphill battle. It's through marketing that you communicate your business's value proposition to potential customers.

Effective marketing strategies help your business achieve several key objectives like customer awareness, customer acquisition, customer retention, market expansion, reputation building.

Entrepreneurial marketing challenges may range from limited resources and market competition to changes in consumer behavior. However, by applying practical strategies and leveraging personal strengths, women entrepreneurs can navigate these challenges effectively.

We won't dwell on the technicalities of marketing that experts have already covered extensively. Instead, we'll focus on empowering you with a fresh perspective and a transformative approach to marketing.

STRATEGY

Believe in Your Business:

It all starts with a genuine belief in your product or service. When you truly believe in what you're offering, this passion and conviction will shine through in your marketing efforts, attracting and inspiring your target audience.

Cost-effectiveness:

If you're working with a tight budget, focus on cost-effective marketing strategies like organic social media marketing, SEO, and email marketing.

Leveraging free or low-cost online tools for content creation, social media scheduling, and customer relationship management can also save costs.

Focus on your uniqueness:

To stand out in a crowded market, emphasize what makes your business unique. This could be your product's unique features, your exceptional customer service, or your brand's commitment to a social cause.

Keeping up with Marketing Trends:

The world of marketing evolves rapidly. Make it a habit to stay updated on the latest marketing trends through online courses, webinars, blogs, and podcasts. Experiment with new strategies, but always keep track of what works and what doesn't for your business.

Learn from Failures:

Not every marketing campaign will be a roaring success, and that's okay. Failures and setbacks aren't signs of weakness; they're invaluable opportunities to learn, adapt, and improve. Embrace these moments as part of your journey to marketing mastery.

Take Care of Yourself:

Entrepreneurship is a marathon, not a sprint. Take care of your physical and mental health. Make time for relaxation, hobbies, and spending time with loved ones. A healthy, balanced entrepreneur is more likely to excel in marketing efforts and business overall.

Leverage Personal Strengths:

As a woman, you bring unique strengths to the table. Your empathy, resilience, multitasking abilities, and collaborative mindset are all assets that can be leveraged in your marketing which can lead to more effective and personalized marketing.

Commitment:

Commitment in marketing is all about showing that you care about your customers and their happiness. By consistently delivering on what you promise and making sure your products or services are top-notch, you build trust and become known as someone reliable. It involves ongoing efforts to engage with customers, understand their evolving needs, and continuously improve their experience. By actively listening to feedback, promptly addressing concerns, and offering personalized solutions, you demonstrate your commitment to their success and well-being. When customers see your commitment, they feel confident that you value them and their needs. It's like giving them a guarantee that you'll always do your best to make them happy.

Content Creation:

Quality content that provides value to your audience can help you build credibility and trust. This can include blogs, videos, podcasts, or infographics that educate, inspire, or entertain. Aim to solve problems or answer questions your audience may have related to your area of expertise.

Growing a business isn't just about quick wins; it's about sustainable, long-term success. Effective marketing and a focus on customer retention can play a significant role in achieving this goal.

KEY LEARNINGS

- Staying updated on the latest marketing trends is crucial to remain competitive.
- High-quality, relevant content not only attracts but also retains customers
- Tailoring marketing messages to individual preferences can significantly boost engagement and conversion rates.
- Maintain a consistent brand image and voice across all marketing channels
- Monitoring and measuring marketing efforts is vital.

ACTIONS

- Identify platforms where your target audience spends most of their time.
- Stay updated with industry developments and market shifts.
- Allocate a budget for different marketing activities.
- Use tools like Google Analytics, Facebook Insights, or email analytics to track performance.

CHAPTER 13

ELEVATE YOUR SALES

"It's no longer about interrupting pitching and closing. It is about listening, diagnosing and prescribing."

- *Mark Roberge*

Sales is the lifeline of any business, acting as the primary driver for growth, profitability, and long-term sustainability. It's not merely about exchanging goods and services for money; sales reflect a business's ability to understand market demands, foster trust with consumers, and successfully position its offerings in a competitive landscape. For woman entrepreneurs, the sales domain brings its own set of unique challenges and strengths. Historically, women have faced systemic biases, ranging from questions about their credibility and capability to balancing societal expectations and professional ambitions. However, many woman entrepreneurs have turned these challenges into strengths.

STRATEGY

Art of listening:

Active listening is not just about hearing the words a customer says, but truly understanding their underlying needs, concerns, and motivations. By focusing intently on the customer and asking open-ended questions, salespeople can glean invaluable insights. This approach allows the seller to tailor their pitch more effectively, making it resonate deeply with the customer's specific situation. Moreover, by demonstrating genuine interest and understanding, trust is fostered, paving the way for a more fruitful sales relationship.

Conveying the value proposition:

Customers don't buy products or services; they buy solutions to their problems. Therefore, it's crucial for salespeople to clearly and compellingly convey the unique value their offering brings. This goes beyond listing features or specifications. Instead, it involves painting a vivid picture of how the product or service will enhance the customer's life or business, addressing their specific pain points, and offering tangible benefits. A strong value proposition differentiates an offering from competitors and compels the customer to act.

Handling objections and converting them into opportunities:

By anticipating common objections and having well-thought-out responses, a salesperson can navigate these moments with confidence. Moreover, each objection provides insights into the customer's priorities and hesitations, allowing for a more tailored and persuasive approach. Embracing objections and using them as stepping stones towards agreement can drastically elevate the sales process. The key is to be prepared.

Relationship building:

Sales have always been about relationships. In a world inundated with choices, people often buy from those they trust. Attending industry conferences, joining professional organizations, or engaging in local business groups can open doors to potential clients and partners. Encouraging satisfied customers to refer others is a cost-effective method to gain new business. Offering referral discounts can incentivize this further. Beyond the immediate sale, maintaining ongoing communication with clients ensures repeat business and potential upsells.

Effective use of sales funnels:

A sales funnel represents the journey a customer takes from first interaction to final purchase. Using targeted advertising, content marketing, and social media to introduce potential customers to your brand. Offering detailed product information, reviews, and comparisons to help prospects evaluate your offering. Streamlined checkout processes, limited time offers, and strong calls to action can turn a prospect into a buyer. After-sales support, loyalty programs, and regular engagement can transform a one-time buyer into a repeat customer.

Diversification:

Relying on a single product, service, or market can be risky. Researching and entering new geographic areas or demographics can tap into fresh customer bases. Introducing complementary products or services can cater to existing customers' broader needs and attract new ones.

Customer retention:

Acquiring a new customer can be five times more expensive than retaining an existing one. Consistently delivering quality products and impeccable service ensures customer satisfaction. Offering rewards for repeat purchases or referrals can encourage repeat business. Regularly soliciting feedback and acting on it shows customers that their opinion matters, fostering a deeper connection.

Emotional intelligence in sales:

In the realm of sales, where building genuine relationships is paramount, EI emerges as an invaluable asset. Women, often societally nurtured to be empathetic and attuned to emotional nuances, frequently exhibit a natural inclination towards high emotional intelligence. In sales scenarios, this means a heightened ability to gauge a customer's mood, understand their unspoken needs, and adapt communication styles to resonate best with the individual. In a market inundated with choices, it's this emotionally intelligent, human touch, often exhibited by women, that can set a brand or product apart.

KEY LEARNINGS

- Recognizing and harnessing unique value proposition in sales pitches can differentiate them from competitors.
- Sales is not just about transactions; it's about building relationships.
- Continuous learning, adapting to market changes, and leveraging new sales tools or platforms can help women entrepreneurs stay ahead of the curve.
- Viewing rejections as learning opportunities, rather than setbacks, can fuel growth and hone sales skills over time.
- By connecting on a deeper, emotional level, sales interactions transform from mere transactions to meaningful engagements.

ACTIONS

- Engage with fresh leads or potential clients every morning.
- Spend a few minutes each day revisiting product features, benefits, and potential objections.
- Allocate time daily to refine your pitch.
- At the end of the day, analyze your sales activities.

Part 5

SUPPORT SYSTEM

CHAPTER 14

BUILDING A STELLAR TEAM

"Teamwork is the secret that makes common people achieve uncommon results"

- Ifeanyi Enoch Onuoha

In the bustling city of Mumbai, Priya had a dream: to open her own organic cafe. The idea sprouted from her love for healthy food and the environment. She had saved up, done her research, and even found the perfect location in Bandra.

However, starting a business was not as easy as she'd imagined. From landlords demanding hefty deposits to suppliers not delivering on time, the challenges were endless. The city, with its fast pace, gave her no time to breathe. The worst part? Priya was all alone in this. Her friends were supportive but too busy in their jobs, and her family, though caring, lived in Delhi and couldn't help much with the on-ground challenges.

One evening, feeling particularly low after a vendor meeting went south, Priya visited a local tea stall. She struck up a conversation with the chaiwala, Rajan, who shared tales of his struggles setting up his tiny stall. His words, "Every start is hard, but with passion, every end can be successful," became her mantra.

Rejuvenated, Priya sought out local business groups for women. Connecting with others like her, she slowly built her support system. Her cafe, 'Mumbai Greens', didn't open overnight, but when it did, it was a testament to her resilience and the community she built.

Women are playing a bigger role in business than ever before. They're starting new companies, leading teams, and making significant changes in all kinds of industries. While their individual talents are impressive, the support of a good team is often what makes a business truly succeed. Simply put, when a business has a strong team that works well together, it grows faster and more effectively. A team, with its combined skills, experiences, and perspectives, often produces results that are greater than what its members could achieve individually; it truly is more than just the sum of its parts. This synergy arises from the complementary strengths of each member, allowing them to address challenges more holistically and innovate more robustly.

STRATEGY

Define clear roles and responsibilities:

Ensure that every team member understands their specific roles, responsibilities, and expectations. Clear delineations prevent overlapping duties and miss tasks, fostering a sense of individual ownership and accountability.

Recognizing and attracting talent:

Woman entrepreneurs should prioritize not just qualifications but also the passion, adaptability, and growth mindset of potential hires. This involves fine-tuning the hiring process, asking insightful questions, and keeping an eye out for raw talent that can be molded and nurtured.

Clear communication and shared vision:

A team that understands the company's mission and their role within that mission is more engaged and driven. Regular team meetings, one-on-ones, and open channels of communication ensure everyone is aligned and moving in the same direction. It's essential for leaders to articulate the bigger picture and show each team member how they fit into that vision.

Investing in continuous learning and development:

The business world is dynamic, with new technologies and methodologies emerging regularly. Prioritize the continuous learning of their team members, offering training sessions, workshops, and courses. This not only upgrades the team's skill set but also demonstrates the leader's commitment to their growth.

Encouraging autonomy and empowerment:

Micro-management can stifle creativity and motivation. By entrusting team members with responsibilities and giving them the autonomy to execute tasks in their own way, entrepreneurs empower them to take ownership and pride in their work. This not only enhances efficiency but also cultivates future leaders within the team.

Celebrating wins and learning from failures:

Recognizing and celebrating both big and small achievements can significantly boost team morale. Equally important is the ability to collectively learn from setbacks without resorting to blame games. A balanced approach to successes and failures fosters resilience and a growth mindset.

Building a culture of trust and accountability:

Mutual trust fosters an environment where team members feel safe to share ideas, take risks, and admit mistakes. By holding individuals accountable, yet being understanding of genuine errors, woman entrepreneurs can build a culture where team members are motivated to deliver their best without fear.

Fostering diversity and inclusion:

Diverse teams bring a myriad of perspectives, leading to richer brainstorming sessions and more holistic solutions. Actively seek individuals from varied backgrounds, genders, ethnicities, and experiences. An inclusive environment where every member feels valued and heard not only boosts morale but also drives innovation.

Address conflicts promptly and constructively:

Differences in opinions, work styles, or personal values can lead to disagreements. Effective resolution lies in fostering an open environment where each member feels heard and understood. Mediation, active listening, and compromise are key components in resolving such disputes. Differences are inevitable in a team setting. Addressing conflicts in their early stages, with a focus on resolution rather than blame, ensures a harmonious and productive team environment.

KEY TAKEAWAYS

- Members should have a clear understanding of their roles and responsibilities.
- When people feel heard and valued, it not only builds trust but also encourages collaboration and innovation.
- Investing in regular training, workshops, and skill-building sessions ensures that the team is always equipped with the latest knowledge and tools to excel.
- Offering flexibility, when possible, can enhance job satisfaction, reduce burnout, and improve overall team productivity.
- Celebrating milestones, big or small, acknowledges efforts and boosts motivation.

ACTIONS

- Host weekly or bi-weekly meetings to keep everyone informed and aligned.
- Encourage team members to take breaks, not overwork, and respect their personal time.
- Organize team activities once a month that will keep them motivated and inspired.

CHAPTER 15

BUILD A TRIBE

"There is immense power when a group of people with similar interests gets together to work toward the same goals."

- Idowu Koyenikan

In the bustling city of Mumbai, Priya had a dream: to open her own organic cafe. The idea sprouted from her love for healthy food and the environment. She had saved up, done her research, and even found the perfect location in Bandra.

However, starting a business was not as easy as she'd imagined. From landlords demanding hefty deposits to suppliers not delivering on time, the challenges were endless. The city, with its fast pace, gave her no time to breathe. The worst part? Priya was all alone in this. Her friends were supportive but too busy in their jobs, and her family, though caring, lived in Delhi and couldn't help much with the on-ground challenges.

One evening, feeling particularly low after a vendor meeting went south, Priya visited a local tea stall. She struck up a conversation with the chaiwala, Rajan, who shared tales of his struggles setting up his tiny stall. His words, "Every start is hard, but with passion, every end can be successful," became her mantra.

Rejuvenated, Priya sought out local business groups for women. Connecting with others like her, she slowly built her support system. Her cafe, 'Mumbai Greens', didn't open overnight, but when it did, it was a testament to her resilience and the community she built.

Being part of a community creates a sense of belonging, a fundamental human need. As social beings, we thrive on connection. A supportive tribe offers camaraderie, reducing feelings of isolation that entrepreneurs often experience. Knowing there are people who support and believe in your ideas can significantly boost your motivation and resilience. During challenging times, your tribe can provide encouragement, keep your spirits high, and help you stay committed to your goals. Positive feedback and validation from your tribe can help build your confidence. Seeing others believe in your vision and abilities can empower you to take risks and make bold decisions. Running a business can be stressful, leading to burnout and other mental health issues. A supportive community can help mitigate these effects by offering empathetic listening, understanding, and stress-management resources.

STRATEGY

Connect:

Women tend to excel in building connections, which can be utilized for partnering with other businesses or influencers in your field to reach a wider audience. Share your experiences, learn from others, and find comfort and inspiration in the knowledge that others are navigating similar challenges.

Authentic storytelling:

Sharing your personal journey, your motivations, and the challenges you've overcome can create a powerful emotional connection with your tribe. This authenticity allows you to attract individuals who identify with your story and want to be part of your journey.

Visibility:

Regular posting on social media can keep you and your business at the top of mind for your tribe. Using search engine optimization (SEO) strategies can also make it easier for potential tribe members to find you online.

Encouragement:

Encouraging continuous learning within your tribe ensures that your community remains up to date with industry trends, new products or services, and any changes within your business. Despite the growth, strive to maintain a personal connection with your community. You could do this by hosting regular live chats, Q&A sessions, or meet-and-greet events.

Collaborative problem solving:

Organize brainstorming sessions or mastermind groups where members can present challenges they're facing and get feedback or solutions from others. This collective problem-solving approach can lead to innovative solutions and deepen community bonds.

Evolution:

As your business and industry evolve, so too should your tribe. This could involve attracting new members, expanding your community's focus, or updating your community's values or mission. This might mean learning new tools, embracing new communication channels, or adapting to new community guidelines.

KEY LEARNINGS

- Build a tribe around genuine connections and shared values.
- Leverage technology and platforms to manage the community effectively.
- Continual learning and adaptability are crucial to ensure your tribe remains engaged and relevant.
- Automate processes wherever possible.
- Establish and enforce clear community guidelines to ensure that all members feel safe and respected.

ACTIONS

- Choose a platform, online or offline, where you want your community to flourish.
- Organize virtual or in-person events, workshops, or meetups to foster connections among community members.
- Regularly feature or spotlight members who are contributing significantly or have compelling stories to share.
- Offer community members special deals, early access, or exclusive content to make them feel valued.

CONCLUSION

This book has been a labour of love. I wrote it for you so that you, too, can experience learnings that have changed my life. These learnings, as profound as they may be, are useless if they are not understood and correctly applied in your life.

As we reach the end of this journey together in "Make It Happen", is a blueprint that begins with unlocking potential and ends with building a tribe, a four-step process that encapsulates the heart and soul of what it means to be a woman entrepreneur.

We discovered that every woman is a reservoir of untapped potential waiting to be released. Our fears are just illusions standing between us and our dreams, and our strengths are our tools to dismantle these illusions. We realized that dreams are not just whimsical thoughts but powerful visions that guide our entrepreneurial journey.

We learned the art of asserting our presence, both online and offline, to let the world know that we are here, ready to make a change. Our personal stories become our tool to connect with our audience, and our authenticity becomes our magnet to attract them.

We understood the importance of showcasing our skills, experiences, and success stories. We discovered that business is not just about selling our products or services; it's about selling our vision, our passion, and our values. Our customer-centric approach, our engaging content, and our strategic promotions became our ladder to success.

We learned to build a community of people who believe in our ideas, who resonate with our values, and who become our loyal customers, our ardent supporters, and our lifelines during challenging times.

Looking back at this transformative journey, it's amazing to see how far we have come. We began with unlocking our potential, and we are now surrounded by a tribe of supporters. Each step of this journey has been a lesson, a challenge, an opportunity, and a milestone.

But remember, the journey doesn't end here. The world of entrepreneurship is an ever-evolving one, and we must keep moving, keep learning and keep adapting. We must remember that every challenge is an opportunity to learn, every failure is a stepping stone to success, and every setback is a call to bounce back with even more determination.

I hope "Make It Happen" has ignited a spark within you, a spark to dream, to dare, to do. The path to success is laid out in front of you, all you need to do is step forward. So, embrace your fears, unleash your potential, and embark on your entrepreneurial journey. You are a woman entrepreneur, and there's nothing you can't achieve!

The world needs you and your unique ideas. There's an audience waiting to hear your story, a market waiting to experience your products or services, a tribe waiting to join your journey. Don't keep them waiting. It's time to step into the spotlight, it's time to make a difference, it's time to make it happen!

And remember, you are not alone. You have your tribe with you - a tribe of fellow women entrepreneurs, a tribe of supporters, and a tribe of people who believe in you. Together, we can create a world where women entrepreneurs are celebrated, respected, and successful. Together, we can make it happen.

As we part ways at the end of this book, I want to leave you with this: Believe in the power of your dreams, for they hold the potential to change your life and the world. You are stronger than your fears, greater than your limitations, and capable of more than you can ever imagine. So, step out of the shadows, embrace your power, and make it happen.

Let's make it happen. Together!

ABOUT THE AUTHOR

As an architect turned coach, consultant, speaker, trainer, and author, Shraddha has seamlessly blended her professional journey with her passionate pursuits.

Her lens captures not just structures but stories, making her a photographer with a unique vision. A travel enthusiast, she believes that exploration fuels inspiration, and her adventures shape her multifaceted worldview.

Shraddha's professional mission is rooted in transformation. Having collaborated with women entrepreneurs and organizations, she has been instrumental in unlocking potentials and guiding them towards the realization of both professional and personal goals. Her growth formula is simple yet powerful: continuous learning is the key, resilience is the path to success, and distancing oneself from those who underestimate is the secret to unfettered achievement.

As an author, Shraddha pens narratives that echo her ethos of empowerment and growth. In her speaking engagements, she shares insights that transcend professional spheres, leaving audiences inspired to navigate their unique paths.